Foreword

In today's fast-paced world, time is precious. \
Shell Scripting in 3 Hours" is designed for the time-conscious individual seeking to quickly grasp the fundamentals of shell scripting.

Within these pages, you'll find a curated collection of essential information presented in a clear, concise, and easily digestible format. Key concepts are explained in a straightforward manner, accompanied by practical examples to solidify your understanding.

Whether you're a system administrator, a developer, or simply curious about automating tasks on your computer, this book provides a valuable starting point. Dive in and discover the power of shell scripting, empowering you to streamline your workflows, increase efficiency, and gain greater control over your system.

Happy scripting!

Re-Wise Publishers

Table of Contents

Chapter 1. Introduction to Shell Scripting

What is Shell Scripting?

- **Definition:**
  - Shell scripting is a powerful technique for automating tasks within a Unix-like operating system (such as Linux, macOS, or BSD).
  - It involves writing scripts using a scripting language interpreted by the shell (like Bash, Zsh, or Sh).

- **Core Concept:**
  - A shell script is essentially a series of commands that the shell executes sequentially.
  - These commands can be any valid shell command, such as commands for file manipulation (copying, moving, renaming), system administration (user management, service control), data processing (filtering, sorting), and more.

- **Key Characteristics:**
  - **Interpreted:** Shell scripts are not compiled like traditional programming languages. The shell reads and executes the script line by line.
  - **Text-Based:** Scripts are written in plain text files, making them easy to create and edit using any text editor.
  - **Leverages Shell Commands:** Scripts utilize the powerful command-line tools available in the operating system (e.g., ls, cp, mv, grep, find, awk, sed).

- **Control Flow:**
  - Scripts support control flow constructs, allowing for more complex logic:
    - **Conditional statements:** if, else, elif - Execute different blocks of code based on conditions.

- **Loops:** for, while, until - Repeat blocks of code a specific number of times or until a condition is met.
- **Functions:** Define reusable blocks of code to improve organization and maintainability.
- **Variables:**
  - Scripts can use variables to store data (e.g., file names, user input), making them more flexible and reusable.
- **Example (Simplified):**

```bash
#!/bin/bash
# This script greets the user

echo "Hello, world!"
echo "What is your name?"
read username
echo "Hello, $username!"
```

This simple script demonstrates: * The #! (shebang) line specifies the interpreter (Bash in this case). * The echo command prints text to the console. * The read command reads input from the user. * Variable substitution (using $username).

In essence, shell scripting provides a way to automate repetitive tasks, streamline workflows, and gain greater control over your operating system by leveraging the power of the shell and its commands.

Why Learn Shell Scripting?

- **Automation:**
  - **Repetitive Tasks:** Automate tedious or time-consuming tasks, such as file manipulation (copying, moving, renaming), backups, user management (creating, deleting, modifying user accounts), and system maintenance (checking disk space, monitoring system logs).
  - **Streamline Workflows:** Create scripts to automate complex workflows, improving efficiency and reducing manual effort. For example, a script could automate the process of

compiling source code, running tests, and deploying the resulting application.

- **System Administration:**
  - **Essential for Sysadmins:** Shell scripting is a core skill for system administrators to manage servers, configure systems, and troubleshoot issues.
  - **Control over Systems:** Gain granular control over your operating system and its components. Scripts can be used to configure network settings, manage services (start, stop, restart), and perform system-level tasks like installing software packages.
- **Development:**
  - **Build and Test:** Automate the build and testing process for software projects. Scripts can be used to compile source code, run unit tests, and perform other tasks in the development cycle.
  - **Deploy Applications:** Script deployments to servers, ensuring consistent and reliable deployments. This can involve tasks like copying files, configuring server settings, and restarting services.
  - **Manage Development Environments:** Set up and manage development environments quickly and easily. Scripts can be used to install necessary software, configure environment variables, and create virtual environments.
- **Data Processing:**
  - **Extract, Transform, and Load (ETL):** Process and transform data from various sources using shell commands and utilities. This can involve extracting data from databases, files, or APIs, transforming the data into the desired format, and loading it into another system.
  - **Data Analysis:** Perform basic data analysis and manipulation tasks. Scripts can be used to filter, sort, and analyze data, and generate reports.
- **Problem-Solving:**

- **Develop Custom Tools:** Create specialized tools and utilities to solve specific problems or automate unique workflows. This can range from simple scripts to perform a specific task to more complex utilities that provide a set of features.
- **Troubleshoot Issues:** Diagnose and resolve system problems more effectively by scripting diagnostic checks and automated solutions. Scripts can be used to gather system information, check logs for errors, and automate the process of resolving common issues.

- **Efficiency:**
  - **Save Time and Effort:** Avoid repetitive manual tasks, freeing up time for more important work.
  - **Reduce Errors:** Minimize the risk of human error by automating tasks. Manual tasks are prone to errors, especially when performed repeatedly. Scripts can ensure that tasks are performed consistently and accurately every time.
  - **Improve Consistency:** Ensure that tasks are performed consistently and reliably every time. Scripts provide a standardized way of performing tasks, reducing the variability that can occur when tasks are performed manually.

- **Learning:**
  - **Deepen Understanding:** Learning shell scripting provides a deeper understanding of how the operating system works. You'll learn about how the shell interacts with the operating system, how commands are executed, and how to use the powerful tools available in the command-line environment.
  - **Expand Your Skills:** Develop valuable and transferable skills that are highly sought after in many IT roles. Shell scripting is a valuable skill for many IT professionals, including system administrators, DevOps engineers, and software developers.

- **Control:**

- **Gain Control over Your Environment:** Take control of your own environment and customize it to your specific needs. Scripts allow you to automate and customize many aspects of your system, making it work more efficiently and effectively for you.
- **Flexibility:** Adapt and customize scripts to fit your changing requirements. Scripts can be easily modified and updated to meet new needs or accommodate changes in your environment.

By learning shell scripting, you can significantly increase your productivity, improve your efficiency, and gain a deeper understanding of your operating system.

Types of Shells

- **Bourne Shell (sh)**
  - The original Unix shell, serving as the foundation for many others.
  - Known for its simplicity and portability.
  - Often used for system scripts and compatibility.
- **Bourne Again Shell (Bash)**
  - The most widely used shell, often the default in Linux distributions.
  - Extends the Bourne Shell with features like command history, job control, and scripting enhancements.
  - Highly customizable and versatile.
- **C Shell (csh)**
  - Designed with C-like syntax, making it more approachable for programmers familiar with C.
  - Features command history, job control, and aliases.
- **Korn Shell (ksh)**
  - Combines features from both Bourne and C shells.

- Known for its scripting capabilities, including advanced features like arrays and functions.
- **Z Shell (zsh)**
  - A powerful and highly customizable shell with extensive features like:
    - Advanced tab completion
    - Spelling correction
    - Plugins and themes
    - Extensive customization options
- **Fish Shell**
  - A modern and user-friendly shell with a focus on ease of use and discoverability.
  - Features include auto-suggestions, syntax highlighting, and consistent command syntax.
- **Dash**
  - A lightweight and efficient shell optimized for scripting and system startup tasks.
  - Known for its speed and minimal resource usage.

These are some of the most common shells used in Unix-like systems. The choice of shell often depends on individual preferences, specific needs, and the desired level of customization.

Basic Shell Commands

- **cd (Change Directory):**
  - Navigates between directories in the file system.
  - cd alone changes to the home directory.
  - cd .. moves one directory level up.
  - cd / moves to the root directory.
  - cd path/to/directory moves to the specified directory.
- **ls (List Directory Contents):**

- Displays a list of files and directories within the current directory.
- ls -l provides a detailed listing with permissions, owner, size, and modification time.
- ls -a displays all files, including hidden files (starting with a dot).

- **pwd (Print Working Directory):**
  - Displays the absolute path of the current directory.

- **mkdir (Make Directory):**
  - Creates a new directory.
  - mkdir directory_name creates a directory named directory_name.

- **rm (Remove):**
  - Deletes files.
  - rm file_name deletes the specified file.
  - **Caution:** Use with care, as rm deletes files permanently.
  - rm -r directory_name recursively deletes a directory and all its contents.

- **cp (Copy):**
  - Copies files or directories.
  - cp source_file destination_file copies source_file to destination_file.
  - cp -r source_directory destination_directory recursively copies a directory and its contents.

- **mv (Move/Rename):**
  - Moves files or directories.
  - mv source_file destination_file moves source_file to destination_file (effectively renaming it).
  - mv source_file destination_directory moves source_file to the specified directory.
  - mv source_directory destination_directory moves a directory and its contents.

These are fundamental commands for navigating the file system and managing files and directories within the shell.

Variables and Data Types in Shell Scripting

Variables

- **Concept:** Variables are named containers that store data within a shell script.
- **Assignment:**
  - Assigned using the = operator.
  - Example: my_variable="Hello, world!"
- **Accessing Value:**
  - Accessed using the $ symbol followed by the variable name.
  - Example: echo $my_variable

Types of Variables

- **Environment Variables:**
  - System-wide variables that affect the behavior of the shell and its processes.
  - Examples: PATH, HOME, USER, SHELL
  - Defined by the system or user and inherited by child processes.
  - Modified using the export command.
  - Example: export MY_ENV_VAR="some_value"
- **User-defined Variables:**
  - Created within a shell script or interactively within the shell.
  - Scope is typically limited to the current shell or script.

Data Types

- **Shell scripting primarily deals with strings.**
- **Implicit Data Typing:**
  - Variables don't have explicit data types.
  - The shell treats most values as strings.
- **Integer Arithmetic:**
  - Can be performed using arithmetic expansion: $((expression))

o Example: result=$((5 + 3))

Key Points

- Variable names are case-sensitive.

- Special characters like $, *, and \ might need to be escaped within variable values.

- Variables can be used within commands, control flow statements, and other parts of a script.

- Understanding variables is fundamental for writing effective and flexible shell scripts.

Sample Shell Script

This script demonstrates the use of basic shell commands, environment variables, user-defined variables, and string manipulation.

- **Purpose:**
    o Greet the user.
    o Display system information (current user, hostname, and operating system).
    o Demonstrate string manipulation (extracting part of a string).

```bash
#!/bin/bash

# Set an environment variable
export GREETING="Welcome to the shell!"

# Set user-defined variables
USER_NAME=$(whoami)
HOSTNAME=$(hostname)
OS_NAME=$(uname -s)

# Display greeting
echo "$GREETING"

# Display system information
echo "User: $USER_NAME"
echo "Hostname: $HOSTNAME"
echo "Operating System: $OS_NAME"

# String manipulation (extracting part of the hostname)
FIRST_PART_HOSTNAME=${HOSTNAME%%.*}
echo "First part of hostname: $FIRST_PART_HOSTNAME"
```

Explanation:

- **Shebang:** #!/bin/bash specifies that the script should be executed by the Bash shell.
- **Environment Variable:**
  - export GREETING="Welcome to the shell!" sets an environment variable named GREETING with the value "Welcome to the shell!". This variable can be accessed by other processes or scripts.
- **User-defined Variables:**
  - USER_NAME=$(whoami) assigns the current username to the USER_NAME variable.
  - HOSTNAME=$(hostname) assigns the hostname to the HOSTNAME variable.
  - OS_NAME=$(uname -s) assigns the operating system name to the OS_NAME variable.
- **Output:** The script uses the echo command to display the greeting message, system information, and the extracted part of the hostname.
- **String Manipulation:**
  - FIRST_PART_HOSTNAME=${HOSTNAME%%.*} extracts the first part of the hostname before the first dot (.). This demonstrates a simple string manipulation technique.

This script provides a basic example of how to use variables, environment variables, and basic shell commands. You can modify and expand it further to perform more complex tasks based on your requirements.

Operators in Shell Scripting

1. Arithmetic Operators:

- **Purpose:** Used for performing mathematical calculations within a script.
- **Syntax:** Typically used within arithmetic expansion: $((expression))
- **Common Operators:**

- o **Addition:** + (e.g., $((5 + 3)))
- o **Subtraction:** - (e.g., $((10 - 4)))
- o **Multiplication:** * (e.g., $((2 * 6)))
- o **Division:** / (e.g., $((15 / 3)))
- o **Modulus (remainder):** % (e.g., $((10 % 3)))

2. Comparison Operators:

- **Purpose:** Used to compare values and make decisions within conditional statements.
- **Syntax:** Typically used within test expressions: [[expression]]
- **Common Operators:**
  - o **Equal:** == (e.g., [[$a == $b]])
  - o **Not Equal:** != (e.g., [[$a != $b]])
  - o **Greater Than:** > (e.g., [[$a -gt $b]])
  - o **Less Than:** < (e.g., [[$a -lt $b]])
  - o **Greater Than or Equal To:** -ge (e.g., [[$a -ge $b]])
  - o **Less Than or Equal To:** -le (e.g., [[$a -le $b]])
  - o **String Comparison:**
    - ▪ == checks for string equality.
    - ▪ != checks for string inequality.
    - ▪ =~ performs pattern matching using regular expressions.

3. Logical Operators:

- **Purpose:** Combine multiple conditions to create more complex expressions.
- **Syntax:** Used within conditional statements and test expressions.
- **Common Operators:**
  - o **AND:** && (both conditions must be true)
  - o **OR:** || (at least one condition must be true)
  - o **NOT:** ! (negates the condition)
  - o Example: [[$a -gt 0 && $b -lt 10]]

Example:

```
if [[ $a -gt 0 && $b -lt 10 ]]; then
  echo "Both conditions are true"
fi
```

Note: The specific syntax and available operators may vary slightly depending on the shell being used.

How to read this book?

Please note that this book must not only be read; it must be used. The readers are encouraged to have a shell ready to code alongside reading. Coding can only be truly learned through practice. What we read will soon be forgotten, but if we code, we will be able to recall what we code.

This book mentions many commands. These commands have additional functionality that can be explored using the man and --help commands. For instance, man grep will display all the available options for the grep command.

Therefore, it is strongly recommended to use man and --help for all the commands discussed in this book from this point forward. Commands like awk, grep, sed, and xargs, in particular, offer a wide range of options to explore.

Chapter 2. Working with Files and Directories

File System Navigation

- **cd (Change Directory):**
    - Navigates to a different location within the file system.
    - cd alone changes to the home directory.
    - cd .. moves one directory level up.
    - cd / moves to the root directory.
    - cd path/to/directory moves to the specified directory.
- **pwd (Print Working Directory):**
    - Displays the absolute path of the current directory.
- **ls (List Directory Contents):**
    - Displays a list of files and directories within the current directory.
    - ls -l provides a detailed listing with permissions, owner, size, and modification time.
    - ls -a displays all files, including hidden files (starting with a dot).

Creating, Deleting, and Renaming Files and Directories

- **Creating Directories:**
    - mkdir directory_name: Creates a new directory with the specified name.
    - mkdir -p path/to/directory: Creates directories recursively, creating any intermediate directories that don't exist.
- **Creating Files:**
    - touch filename: Creates an empty file.
    - > filename: Creates a new file and overwrites any existing content.
    - echo "some text" > filename: Creates a file and writes the specified text to it.
- **Deleting Files:**

- o rm filename: Deletes the specified file.
    - **Caution:** Use with care, as rm deletes files permanently.
- o rm -r directory_name: Recursively deletes a directory and all its contents.
    - **Caution:** Use with extreme caution, as this cannot be easily undone.
- **Deleting Directories:**
    - o rmdir directory_name: Deletes an empty directory.
    - o rm -r directory_name: Recursively deletes a directory and all its contents.
- **Renaming Files and Directories:**
    - o mv source_file destination_file: Renames source_file to destination_file.
    - o mv source_file destination_directory: Moves source_file to the specified directory.
    - o mv source_directory destination_directory: Moves a directory and its contents.

Sample Code:

```
# Create a new directory
mkdir my_new_directory

# Create a file named "my_file.txt"
touch my_new_directory/my_file.txt

# Write some text to the file
echo "This is a sample text." > my_new_directory/my_file.txt

# Rename the file
mv my_new_directory/my_file.txt my_new_directory/new_filename.txt

# Delete the file
rm my_new_directory/new_filename.txt

# Remove the directory (if empty)
rmdir my_new_directory
```

This script demonstrates how to create, delete, and rename files and directories using basic shell commands. Remember to use these commands with caution, especially when deleting files or directories, as data loss can occur.

Finding Files

- **find command:**
    - Powerful tool for searching for files within the file system based on various criteria.
    - **Basic Usage:** find [path] [options]
    - **Common Options:**
        - -name: Find files with a specific name or pattern (e.g., find . -name "*.txt").
        - -type: Find files of a specific type (e.g., -type f for files, -type d for directories).
        - -size: Find files of a specific size (e.g., -size +10M for files larger than 10MB).
        - -user: Find files owned by a specific user.
        - -group: Find files owned by a specific group.
        - -mtime: Find files modified within a certain time frame.
        - -exec: Execute a command on each found file.
- **grep command:**
    - Searches for patterns within the content of files.
    - **Basic Usage:** grep [options] pattern [files]
    - **Common Options:**
        - -r: Recursively search through directories.
        - -i: Ignore case.
        - -v: Invert the match (find lines that *do not* match the pattern).
        - -c: Count the number of matching lines.
        - -l: List only the names of files that contain a match.

For instance

Find all files ending with ".txt" in the current directory and its subdirectories using
find . -name "*.txt"

Find all files larger than 1MB in the current directory using
find . -size +1M

Find all files owned by the user "root" using
find / -user root

Search for the word "hello" in all files in the current directory and its subdirectories using
grep -r "hello" .

Search for lines that do not contain the word "error" in the file "my_log.txt" use
grep -v "error" my_log.txt

File Permissions

- **Permissions:**
  - Control who can access and modify files and directories.
  - Defined by three sets of permissions:
    - **Owner:** Permissions for the user who owns the file or directory.
    - **Group:** Permissions for users belonging to the same group as the file or directory.
    - **Others:** Permissions for all other users on the system.
  - Each set consists of three permissions:
    - **Read (r):** Allows reading the contents of the file or directory.
    - **Write (w):** Allows writing to the file or modifying the directory.

- **Execute (x):** Allows executing the file (if it's a script or executable) or entering the directory.
- **chmod (Change Mode):**
  - Modifies file permissions.
  - **Syntax:** chmod [options] mode file1 file2 ...
  - **Options:**
    - -R: Recursively change permissions for files and directories within a directory.
  - **Mode:**
    - **Octal notation:**
      - Represents permissions using a three-digit octal number.
      - Each digit represents permissions for owner, group, and others, respectively.
      - Example: 755 (owner: read, write, execute; group: read, execute; others: read, execute)
    - **Symbolic notation:**
      - Uses letters to represent permissions (e.g., u+x to add execute permission for the owner).
- **chown (Change Owner):**
  - Changes the owner of a file or directory.
  - **Syntax:** chown user:group file1 file2 ...
  - Example: chown user1:group1 myfile.txt
- **chgrp (Change Group):**
  - Changes the group ownership of a file or directory.
  - **Syntax:** chgrp group file1 file2 ...
  - Example: chgrp group1 myfile.txt

Sample Code:

```
# Add execute permission for the owner of the file "my_script.sh"
chmod u+x my_script.sh

# Set permissions to read, write, and execute for owner, read and execute for group
chmod 755 my_directory

# Change the owner of "myfile.txt" to "user1"
chown user1 myfile.txt

# Change the group ownership of "myfile.txt" to "group1"
chgrp group1 myfile.txt
```

This script demonstrates how to use chmod, chown, and chgrp to manage file permissions and ownership. Proper file permissions are crucial for system security and data integrity.

Working with Archives

- **Archiving:**
    - The process of compressing and bundling multiple files and directories into a single archive file.
    - Reduces storage space and facilitates easier transfer and backup.
- **tar (Tape Archive):**
    - A versatile command-line utility for creating, extracting, and manipulating archive files.
    - **Common Options:**
        - -c: Create a new archive.
        - -x: Extract files from an archive.
        - -t: List the contents of an archive.
        - -z: Compress/decompress with gzip.
        - -j: Compress/decompress with bzip2.
        - -f: Specify the name of the archive file.
        - -v: Display verbose output.
    - **Examples:**
        - tar -czvf my_archive.tar.gz file1 file2 directory1 (Create a gzip-compressed archive)

- tar -xvf my_archive.tar (Extract files from a tar archive)
- **gzip (GNU Zip):**
  - A popular compression utility for individual files.
  - **Common Options:**
    - -c: Compress a file to standard output.
    - -d: Decompress a gzip file.
    - -f: Force overwrite of existing files.
  - **Examples:**
    - gzip myfile.txt (Compress myfile.txt to myfile.txt.gz)
    - gzip -d myfile.txt.gz (Decompress myfile.txt.gz)
- **bzip2:**
  - Another compression utility that often provides higher compression ratios than gzip.
  - **Common Options:**
    - -c: Compress a file to standard output.
    - -d: Decompress a bzip2 file.
  - **Examples:**
    - bzip2 myfile.txt (Compress myfile.txt to myfile.txt.bz2)
    - bzip2 -d myfile.txt.bz2 (Decompress myfile.txt.bz2)

Sample Code:

```
# Create a gzip-compressed archive of all files in the current directory
tar -czvf my_archive.tar.gz *

# Extract files from the archive
tar -xvf my_archive.tar.gz

# Compress a single file using gzip
gzip myfile.txt

# Decompress the file
gzip -d myfile.txt.gz
```

This script demonstrates how to create, extract, and manipulate archive files using tar, gzip, and bzip2. Archiving is essential for efficient storage and transfer of files.

Chapter 3. Input/Output

Opening Files
- less:
  - A pager that displays the contents of a file one screen at a time.
  - Allows you to easily navigate through large files using commands like:
    - h: Display help.
    - j: Scroll down one line.
    - k: Scroll up one line.
    - b: Scroll back one page.
    - f: Scroll forward one page.
    - q: Quit less.
- vim:
  - A powerful and highly customizable text editor.
  - Can be used for both editing and viewing files.
  - Has two modes:
    - **Command Mode:** Used for navigation, editing commands, and saving.
    - **Insert Mode:** Used for typing text.
  - Offers a steep learning curve but provides immense flexibility and power.
- gvim:
  - The graphical user interface version of vim.
  - Provides a more user-friendly interface with menus and toolbars.
- nano:
  - A simple and easy-to-use text editor.
  - Provides on-screen help and keybindings for common editing tasks.
- cat:

- o Displays the entire contents of a file to the console.
- o Can also be used to create or append to files.

Sample Usage:
- less myfile.txt
- vim myfile.txt
- gvim myfile.txt
- nano myfile.txt
- cat myfile.txt

These commands provide various ways to open and view files in the terminal. The choice of which command to use depends on your preferences and the specific task you are trying to accomplish.

Reading User Input

- **read Command:**
  - o Reads input from the user's keyboard and stores it in a variable.
  - o **Syntax:** read variable_name
- **Example:**
  - o read username
    - ▪ This command will prompt the user to enter input from the keyboard.
    - ▪ The entered text will be stored in the variable username.
- **Multiple Variables:**
  - o The read command can read input for multiple variables.
  - o **Syntax:** read variable1 variable2 variable3
    - ▪ The user will be prompted to enter multiple values separated by spaces.
    - ▪ The first value will be assigned to variable1, the second to variable2, and so on.
- **Prompts:**
  - o You can provide a prompt to the user before reading input.

- o **Syntax:** echo "Enter your name:"
  - read username
- **Reading a Single Line of Input:**
  - o The read command typically reads a single line of input.

Sample Code:

```
#!/bin/bash

echo "Enter your first name:"
read first_name

echo "Enter your last name:"
read last_name

echo "Hello, $first_name $last_name!"
```

This script prompts the user to enter their first and last names, reads the input, and then displays a personalized greeting.

The read command is essential for creating interactive shell scripts that can gather input from the user and customize their behavior accordingly.

Writing Output to the Console

- **echo Command:**
  - o The most common way to display text on the console.
  - o **Syntax:** echo "text to display"
  - o Can display variables using the $ symbol.
  - o Example: echo "Hello, $user"
- **printf Command:**
  - o More versatile than echo for formatted output.
  - o Uses format specifiers (similar to those in C) to control the output.
  - o **Syntax:** printf "format string" argument1 argument2 ...
  - o Example:
    - printf "The value of pi is %.2f\n" 3.14159 (prints "The value of pi is 3.14")
- **printf Format Specifiers:**

- o %s: String
- o %d: Integer
- o %f: Floating-point number
- o \n: Newline character
- o \t: Tab character
- **Redirecting Output:**
  - o **>:** Redirects output to a file.
  - o **>>:** Appends output to a file.
  - o Example:
    - echo "Hello" > output.txt (writes "Hello" to the file output.txt)
    - echo "World" >> output.txt (appends "World" to the file output.txt)

Sample Code:

```bash
#!/bin/bash

user="John Doe"
age=30

echo "Hello, $user!"

printf "Your age is: %d years old.\n" $age

# Redirect output to a file
echo "This message will be written to a file." > output.txt
```

This script demonstrates how to use echo and printf to display output on the console, and how to redirect output to a file.

Redirecting Input/Output

- **> (Output Redirection):**
  - o Directs the standard output of a command to a file.
  - o Example: ls > file_list.txt (Lists directory contents and saves the output to file_list.txt)

- **>> (Output Appending):**
  - ○ Appends the standard output of a command to an existing file.
  - ○ Example: echo "New line" >> my_file.txt (Adds "New line" to the end of my_file.txt)
- **< (Input Redirection):**
  - ○ Directs the standard input of a command from a file.
  - ○ Example: sort < data.txt (Sorts the contents of data.txt)
- **2>&1 (Redirect Standard Error to Standard Output):**
  - ○ Combines standard output and standard error into a single stream.
  - ○ Often used when redirecting both output types to a file.
  - ○ Example: my_command 2>&1 > output.log (Redirects both standard output and standard error to output.log)
- **&> (Redirect Both Standard Output and Standard Error):**
  - ○ A shorthand for 2>&1 >.
  - ○ Example: my_command &> output.log (Same as my_command 2>&1 > output.log)

Examples :

Redirect the output of the `ls` command to a file using
ls > file_list.txt

Append the output of the `date` command to the file using
date >> file_list.txt

Sort the contents of a file and display the result on the console using
sort < data.txt

Run a command and redirect both standard output and standard error to a log file using
my_command &> command.log

Pipes (|)

- **Purpose:**
  - Connect the standard output of one command to the standard input of another command.
  - Allows for creating complex command pipelines.
- **Syntax:**
  - command1 | command2
- **How it works:**
  - command1 executes and sends its output to the standard output.
  - The output of command1 is then automatically fed as input to command2.
- **Example:**
  - ls -l | grep "my_file.txt"
    - This command lists files in the current directory with ls -l.
    - The output of ls -l is then piped to grep, which searches for lines containing "my_file.txt".
- **Chaining Commands:**
  - You can chain multiple commands together using pipes.
  - Example:
    - find . -name "*.txt" | xargs cat
      - This command finds all files ending with ".txt" in the current directory and its subdirectories.
      - The output of find (a list of filenames) is piped to xargs, which executes the cat command on each filename, effectively displaying the contents of all found .txt files.

Example:

List all files in the current directory and pipe the output to `grep` to find files ending with ".log" using
ls | grep ".log"

Find all files ending with ".txt" and pipe the output to `wc -l` to count the number of files using
find . -name "*.txt" | wc -l

Find all files ending with ".txt" and pipe the output to `xargs` to display the contents of each file using
find . -name "*.txt" | xargs cat

Reading from Files

- **cat Command:**
  - Displays the entire contents of a file to the console.
  - cat filename
- **head Command:**
  - Displays the first few lines of a file.
  - head -n 5 filename (displays the first 5 lines)
- **tail Command:**
  - Displays the last few lines of a file.
  - tail -n 10 filename (displays the last 10 lines)
- **less Command:**
  - Displays the contents of a file page by page, allowing you to scroll through it easily.
  - Provides options for searching, filtering, and highlighting text.
- **grep Command:**
  - Searches for specific patterns within the contents of a file.
  - grep "pattern" filename
- awk

- **Pattern Scanning and Text Processing Language:**

- Powerful tool for manipulating text data.
- Reads input line by line, divides each line into fields (usually by whitespace), and performs actions based on patterns or conditions.
- **Basic Syntax:**
  - awk '{ actions }' file
  - awk 'pattern { actions }' file
- **Key Concepts:**
  - **Fields:** Each line is divided into fields, numbered from 1.
    - $1: first field, $2: second field, and so on.
    - $0: represents the entire line.
  - **Patterns:**
    - Can be regular expressions to match specific patterns in the input.
    - Can be conditions to filter lines based on certain criteria.
  - **Actions:**
    - Code blocks enclosed in {} that are executed when a pattern matches.
    - Common actions include:
      - Printing fields (print)
      - Performing calculations
      - Assigning values to variables
- **Built-in Variables:**
  - $0: The entire current line.
  - $1, $2, ...: Individual fields within the current line.
  - NF: Number of fields in the current line.
  - NR: Record number (line number).
  - FS: Field separator (default is whitespace).

- sed

- **Stream Editor:**

- o Reads input line by line and performs text transformations.
- o Can be used for various tasks like:
  - Substituting text
  - Deleting lines
  - Inserting lines
  - Printing specific lines
- **Basic Syntax:**
  - o sed 'command' file
- **Common Commands:**
  - o s/old/new/: Substitute old with new.
    - s/old/new/g: Substitute all occurrences of old with new.
  - o d: Delete the current line.
  - o p: Print the current line.
  - o a\text: Append text to the current line.
  - o i\text: Insert text before the current line.
- **Example:**
  - o sed 's/old/new/g' file.txt: Replace all occurrences of "old" with "new" in file.txt.
  - o sed '2d' file.txt: Delete the second line of file.txt.
  - o sed '/pattern/d' file.txt: Delete lines that match the pattern.

Key Differences

- **Focus:**
  - o awk is primarily designed for data processing and analysis.
  - o sed is primarily designed for text editing and manipulation.
- **Approach:**
  - o awk focuses on dividing lines into fields and performing actions based on field values.
  - o sed focuses on manipulating lines of text using regular expressions and commands.

Both awk and sed are powerful tools for text processing. The choice of which tool to use depends on the specific task at hand.

For example to
display the contents of a file use
cat my_file.txt

To display the first 10 lines of a file use
head -n 10 my_file.txt

To display the last 5 lines of a file use
tail -n 5 my_file.txt

To search for the word "keyword" in a file use
grep "keyword" my_file.txt

This script demonstrates how to read and display the contents of files using various commands. These commands are essential for working with text files and extracting information from them.

Writing to Files

- **echo with Redirection:**
  - echo "text" > filename: Overwrites the contents of filename with the given text.
  - echo "text" >> filename: Appends the text to the end of filename.
- **printf with Redirection:**
  - printf "format string" arguments > filename
  - Formats and writes the output to the file.
- **tee Command:**
  - Displays output on the console and also writes it to a file simultaneously.
  - command | tee output.txt
- **cat with Redirection:**
  - cat > filename
    - Creates a new file and allows you to enter text from the keyboard.

- Press Ctrl+D to save and exit.
- **Using a Loop to Write Multiple Lines:**
    - You can use a loop to write multiple lines of text to a file.

For example

Write a single line to a file using
echo "This is the first line." > my_file.txt

Append another line to the file using
echo "This is the second line." >> my_file.txt

Write formatted output to a file using
printf "The value of pi is %.2f\n" 3.14159 > pi_value.txt

Run a command and display the output on the console while also writing it to a file using
ls -l | tee output.txt

Chapter 4. Control Flow

If-Then-Else Statements

- **Purpose:**
    - Control the flow of execution in a script based on conditions.
    - Allow you to execute different blocks of code depending on whether a certain condition is true or false.
- **Basic Syntax:**

if [condition]; then
  # Commands to execute if the condition is true
fi

- **Adding else:**

if [condition]; then
  # Commands to execute if the condition is true
else
  # Commands to execute if the condition is false
fi

- **Adding elif (else if):**

if [condition1]; then
  # Commands to execute if condition1 is true
elif [condition2]; then
  # Commands to execute if condition1 is false and condition2 is true
else
  # Commands to execute if neither condition1 nor condition2 is true
fi

- **Conditions:**
    - Typically enclosed within [and] (or [[ ]] for more advanced comparisons).
    - Use comparison operators (e.g., ==, !=, -gt, -lt, -eq, -ne) to test conditions.
    - Example:

- [$a -gt $b] (checks if the value of variable a is greater than the value of variable b)

Sample Code:

```bash
#!/bin/bash

# Get user input
read -p "Enter a number: " number

# Check if the number is positive, negative, or zero
if [ $number -gt 0 ]; then
   echo "The number is positive."
elif [ $number -lt 0 ]; then
   echo "The number is negative."
else
   echo "The number is zero."
fi
```

This script demonstrates how to use if, elif, and else statements to check the value of a number and display an appropriate message.

Case Statements

- **Purpose:**
  - Provide a way to execute different blocks of code based on the value of a variable or expression.
  - Offers a more concise way to handle multiple conditions compared to nested if-elif-else statements.
- **Basic Syntax:**

```
case "$variable" in
  "value1")
    # Commands to execute if $variable is equal to "value1"
    ;;
  "value2")
    # Commands to execute if $variable is equal to "value2"
    ;;
```

```
*)
```
Commands to execute if $variable does not match any of the specified values

```
    ;;
esac
```

- **Key Points:**
  - $variable is the variable or expression to be evaluated.
  - Each case option is followed by), the code to be executed, and ;;.
  - The *) pattern is optional and acts as a default case.
  - Strings are usually enclosed in double quotes (") for proper handling of spaces and special characters.

Sample Code:

```bash
#!/bin/bash

echo "Enter a fruit:"
read fruit

case "$fruit" in
    "apple")
        echo "An apple a day keeps the doctor away."
        ;;
    "banana")
        echo "Bananas are a good source of potassium."
        ;;
    "orange")
        echo "Oranges are rich in vitamin C."
        ;;
    *)
        echo "I don't know about that fruit."
        ;;
esac
```

This script prompts the user to enter a fruit and then displays a message based on the entered fruit. This demonstrates the basic usage of a case statement to handle different scenarios.

Loops
- **Purpose:**
  - ○ Repeatedly execute a block of code.
  - ○ Used to automate tasks that require iteration or repetition.
- **for Loop:**
  - ○ Iterates over a sequence of values.
  - ○ **Syntax:**
    - ▪ for variable in list; do commands done
  - ○ list can be:
    - ▪ A sequence of values separated by spaces.
    - ▪ A range of numbers (e.g., for i in {1..10}; do ...; done)
    - ▪ The output of another command.
- **while Loop:**
  - ○ Repeats a block of code as long as a given condition is true.
  - ○ **Syntax:**
    - ▪ while [condition]; do commands done
- **until Loop:**
  - ○ Repeats a block of code as long as a given condition is false.
  - ○ **Syntax:**
    - ▪ until [condition]; do commands done

Sample Code:

```bash
#!/bin/bash

# for loop
echo "Counting from 1 to 5:"
for i in {1..5}; do
    echo $i
done

# while loop
counter=0
while [ $counter -lt 5 ]; do
    echo $counter
    ((counter++))
done

# until loop
counter=0
until [ $counter -eq 5 ]; do
    echo $counter
    ((counter++))
done
```

This script demonstrates the use of for, while, and until loops to perform simple iterations.

Break and Continue Statements
- **Purpose:**
    - Control the flow of execution within loops.
- **break Statement:**
    - Immediately exits the current loop.
    - Useful for terminating the loop prematurely based on a certain condition.
- **continue Statement:**
    - Skips the remaining portion of the current iteration of the loop.
    - The loop then proceeds to the next iteration.

Sample Code:

```bash
#!/bin/bash

# for loop with break
for i in {1..10}; do
  if [ $i -eq 5 ]; then
    break
  fi
  echo $i
done

# for loop with continue
for i in {1..10}; do
  if [ $((i % 2)) -eq 0 ]; then
    continue  # Skip even numbers
  fi
  echo $i
done
```

This script demonstrates how to use break and continue statements to control the flow of execution within loops. The first loop breaks out of the loop when the value of i reaches 5. The second loop skips even numbers and only prints odd numbers.

Chapter 5. Scripting Utilities

Working with Text

- **cut:**
  - Extracts selected portions of lines from a file.
  - **Options:**
    - -d: Specify the delimiter (default is tab).
    - -f: Specify the fields to extract (e.g., -f1 for the first field, -f1,3 for the first and third fields).
  - Useful for extracting specific columns from data files.

- **paste:**
  - Joins lines from multiple files or from the standard input.
  - Can be used to combine data from different sources.

- **sed (Stream Editor):**
  - Powerful tool for manipulating text data.
  - Can be used for:
    - **Substitution:** Replacing patterns of text (e.g., s/old/new/g to replace all occurrences of "old" with "new").
    - **Deletion:** Deleting lines or parts of lines.
    - **Insertion:** Inserting text at specific locations.
    - **Filtering:** Selecting lines based on patterns.

- **awk:**
  - A pattern-scanning and text-processing language.
  - Can be used for:
    - **Field extraction:** Dividing lines into fields and extracting specific fields.
    - **Data filtering:** Selecting lines based on conditions.
    - **Data manipulation:** Performing calculations, formatting data, and generating reports.
    - **Pattern matching:** Using regular expressions to find and process specific patterns.

Sample Code:

```
# Extract the second field (delimited by commas) from a file
cut -d',' -f2 data.csv

# Join the contents of two files line by line
paste file1.txt file2.txt

# Replace all occurrences of "old" with "new" in a file
sed 's/old/new/g' data.txt

# Print the first field of each line in a file
awk '{print $1}' data.txt
```

This script demonstrates basic usage of cut, paste, sed, and awk for working with text data.

Date and Time Commands

- **date:**
    - Displays the current date and time.
    - Offers various options for formatting and manipulating date and time information.
    - **Common Options:**
        - -d "YYYY-MM-DD": Display the date for a specific date.
        - -r: Display the date in readable format.
        - +%Y: Display the year (e.g., 2024).
        - +%m: Display the month (01-12).
        - +%d: Display the day of the month (01-31).
        - +%H: Display the hour in 24-hour format (00-23).
        - +%M: Display the minute (00-59).
        - +%S: Display the second (00-59).
- **cal:**
    - Displays a calendar for a specific month or year.
    - **Usage:**
        - cal: Displays the current month.

- cal <month> <year>: Displays the calendar for a specific month and year.

For instance
To display the current date and time use
date

Display the date in a specific format (YYYY-MM-DD)
date +%Y-%m-%d using

Display the date for a specific date
date -d "2024-12-25"

Display the calendar for the current month using
cal

Display the calendar for July 2024 using
cal 7 2024

This script demonstrates the basic usage of the date and cal commands for displaying and manipulating date and time information.

File Comparison Tools
- **diff:**
  - Compares two files line by line and displays the differences between them.
  - **Output:**
    - Shows the lines that are added, deleted, or changed in the second file compared to the first.
    - Uses special characters to indicate the type of change (e.g., < for lines deleted from file1, > for lines added to file2).
- **cmp:**
  - Compares two files byte by byte.

- o **Output:**
    - If the files are identical, no output is produced.
    - If differences are found, displays the byte offset where the first difference occurs.

Example

Compare two files and display the differences using
diff file1.txt file2.txt

Compare two files byte by byte using
cmp file1.txt file2.txt

This script demonstrates the basic usage of diff and cmp for comparing files. These tools are useful for identifying changes between versions of files, such as code files, configuration files, or any other type of text file.

Network Commands

- **ping:**
    - o Sends ICMP (Internet Control Message Protocol) echo request packets to a target host.
    - o Used to test network connectivity and measure round-trip time (RTT).
    - o **Options:**
        - -c count: Specify the number of packets to send.
        - -i interval: Specify the interval between packets.
        - -w timeout: Specify the timeout for each request.
- **nslookup:**
    - o Queries a DNS (Domain Name System) server to resolve domain names to IP addresses and vice versa.
    - o Can also be used to get other DNS information, such as mail exchanger records (MX) and name server records (NS).
- **wget:**
    - o Downloads files from the internet.
    - o Supports various protocols, including HTTP, HTTPS, FTP, and more.

- Options:
  - -O filename: Specify the output filename.
  - -c: Continue a previously interrupted download.
  - -r: Recursively download files from a website.

Example

Ping the Google website using
ping google.com

Resolve the IP address of www.example.com using
nslookup www.example.com

Download a file from the internet using
wget https://example.com/file.zip

This script demonstrates the basic usage of ping, nslookup, and wget for network operations. These commands are essential for troubleshooting network connectivity, resolving domain names, and downloading files from the internet.

User and Group Management

- **useradd:**
  - Creates a new user account.
  - **Options:**
    - -m: Create the user's home directory.
    - -g group: Specify the primary group for the user.
    - -G group1,group2: Specify additional groups for the user.
    - -p password: Set the user's password (not recommended for security reasons).
- **userdel:**
  - Deletes a user account.
  - **Options:**
    - -r: Remove the user's home directory.
- **groupadd:**
  - Creates a new group.

- **groupdel:**
  - Deletes a group.
- **passwd:**
  - Changes the password for a user.
- **su:**
  - Switch to another user account.
- **sudo:**
  - Execute commands with the privileges of another user, typically the root user.

Sample Code:

```
# Create a new user named "newuser" with the home directory created
useradd -m newuser

# Add the user "newuser" to the "sudo" group
usermod -aG sudo newuser

# Delete the user "newuser" and remove the home directory
userdel -r newuser

# Create a new group named "mygroup"
groupadd mygroup

# Delete the group "mygroup"
groupdel mygroup
```

This script demonstrates basic user and group management commands. Remember to use these commands with caution and follow security best practices.

xargs

- **Purpose:**
  - Reads input from standard input and executes a specified command with each input item as an argument.
- **Usage:**
  - xargs command

- **Key Features:**
  - **Processing Output from Other Commands:**
    - Often used to process the output of other commands as arguments for another command.
    - Example: find . -name "*.txt" | xargs cat (reads the output of find, which is a list of filenames, and executes cat on each filename).
  - **Handling Long Command Lines:**
    - Avoids the limitations of the command-line length by breaking down long lists of arguments into multiple command invocations.
  - **Options:**
    - -n: Specify the number of arguments to pass to the command in each invocation.
    - -I: Specify a placeholder string to be replaced with each input item.
    - -L: Specify the number of lines to read from standard input before invoking the command.

Sample Code:

```
# Find all files ending with ".txt" and display their contents
find . -name "*.txt" | xargs cat

# Find all files ending with ".txt" and count the number of lines in each file
find . -name "*.txt" | xargs wc -l

# Rename all files ending with ".txt" to ".log"
find . -name "*.txt" | xargs -I {} mv {} {}.log
```

This script demonstrates the use of xargs to process the output of other commands, such as find, and to execute commands with multiple arguments. xargs is a powerful tool for automating tasks that involve processing large amounts of data.

Chapter 6. Functions

Defining Functions

- **Purpose:**
  - ○ Encapsulate a block of code that performs a specific task.
  - ○ Improve code organization, readability, and reusability.
- **Syntax:**

```
function function_name() {
 # Commands to be executed within the function
}
```

- **Calling a Function:**
  - ○ function_name
- **Passing Arguments:**
  - ○ Functions can accept arguments.
  - ○ Access arguments within the function using $1, $2, $3, etc.
  - ○ $0 represents the name of the script itself.
- **Returning Values:**
  - ○ Functions can return values using the return statement.
  - ○ The returned value can be assigned to a variable.

Sample Code:

```bash
#!/bin/bash

# Define a function to greet the user
function greet() {
  echo "Hello, $1!"
}

# Call the function
greet "John Doe"

# Define a function to add two numbers
function add() {
  echo $(($1 + $2))
}

# Call the function and store the result in a variable
result=$(add 5 3)
echo "The sum is: $result"
```

This script demonstrates how to define and call functions, pass arguments to functions, and return values from functions. Functions are essential for writing well-structured and maintainable shell scripts.

Function Arguments

- **Passing Arguments:**
    - Functions can accept input values called arguments.
    - Arguments are passed to the function when it is called.
- **Accessing Arguments:**
    - Within a function, arguments are accessed using positional parameters:
        - $1: The first argument.
        - $2: The second argument.
        - $3: The third argument, and so on.
    - $0: Represents the name of the script itself.
    - $@: Represents all arguments as a single word.
    - $*: Represents all arguments as a single string.
- **Example:**

```
function greet() {
  echo "Hello, $1 $2!"   # Accesses the first and second arguments
}

greet "John" "Doe"
```

- **Special Parameters:**
    - $#: Represents the number of arguments passed to the function.
    - $*: Represents all arguments as a single string.
    - $@: Represents all arguments as individual strings.

Sample Code:

```bash
#!/bin/bash

function sum() {
   local result=0
   for i in "$@"; do
      ((result+=i))
   done
   echo $result
}

result=$(sum 10 20 30)
echo "Sum: $result"
```

This script demonstrates how to pass arguments to a function and access them within the function. The sum function calculates the sum of all the arguments passed to it.

Return Values

- **Returning a Value:**
  - Functions can return a value to the calling part of the script.
  - Use the return statement followed by the value to be returned.
- **Accessing the Returned Value:**
  - The returned value can be captured and used in other parts of the script.
  - Typically, the return value is captured in a variable.
- **Example:**

```bash
function multiply() {
   local result=$(($1 * $2))
   return $result
}

# Call the function and store the returned value in a variable
result=$(multiply 5 3)

echo "The product is: $result"
```

- **Important Notes:**
  - The return statement can only return an integer value.
  - To return other data types (strings, floating-point numbers), you can use echo within the function and capture the output.

Sample Code:

```bash
#!/bin/bash

function get_filename() {
  local filename="my_file.txt"
  return $filename
}

# Call the function and store the returned filename
file=$(get_filename)

echo "Filename: $file"
```

This script demonstrates how to return a value from a function and how to capture that returned value in a variable. This is a fundamental concept for writing more complex and modular shell scripts.

Scope of Variables
- **Local Variables:**
  - Declared within a function using the local keyword.
  - Only accessible within that specific function.
  - Changes made to a local variable within a function do not affect variables with the same name outside the function.

- **Global Variables:**
  - Declared outside any function.
  - Accessible from anywhere within the script, including within functions.
  - Changes made to a global variable within a function affect the variable's value throughout the script.

- **Example:**

```
global_var=10

function my_function() {
    local local_var=5
    echo "Inside function:"
    echo "Global variable: $global_var"
    echo "Local variable: $local_var"
    global_var=20  # Modifies the global variable
}

echo "Before function call:"
echo "Global variable: $global_var"

my_function

echo "After function call:"
echo "Global variable: $global_var"
```

Explanation:

1. **global_var:** This is a global variable, declared outside the function.
2. **local_var:** This is a local variable, declared within the my_function. It is only accessible within that function.
3. Inside the function, we modify both the global and local variables.
4. After the function call, the value of the global variable has changed, while the local variable is no longer accessible.

This script demonstrates the concept of local and global variables and how their scope affects their accessibility and behavior within a shell script.

Chapter 7. Arrays

Creating Arrays
- **Definition:**
  - An array is a collection of ordered values.
  - In shell scripting, arrays can store multiple values within a single variable.
- **Creating an Array:**
  - **Method 1:**
    - array_name=(value1 value2 value3)
  - **Method 2:**
    - Assign values to individual elements of the array:
      - array_name[0]="value1"
      - array_name[1]="value2"
      - array_name[2]="value3"
- **Accessing Array Elements:**
  - echo ${array_name[index]}
    - index starts from 0 (for the first element).
- **Accessing All Elements:**
  - echo ${array_name[@]}
- **Getting Array Length:**
  - echo ${#array_name[@]}

Below script demonstrates how to create arrays, access individual elements, access all elements, and get the number of elements in an array. Arrays are a powerful feature in shell scripting that allows you to work with collections of data efficiently.

Sample Code:

```bash
#!/bin/bash

# Create an array using method 1
fruits=("apple" "banana" "orange")

# Access individual elements
echo "First fruit: ${fruits[0]}"
echo "Second fruit: ${fruits[1]}"

# Access all elements
echo "All fruits: ${fruits[@]}"

# Get the number of elements in the array
echo "Number of fruits: ${#fruits[@]}"

# Create an array using method 2
colors[0]="red"
colors[1]="green"
colors[2]="blue"

# Access the second element
echo "Second color: ${colors[1]}"
```

Array Operations

- **Adding Elements:**
  - **Append:**
    - array_name+=("new_value")
  - **Insert at a specific index:**
    - array_name[index]="new_value"
- **Removing Elements:**
  - **Remove a specific element:**
    - unset array_name[index]
  - **Clear the entire array:**
    - unset array_name[@]
- **Iterating through an Array:**
  - **Using a for loop:**
    - for element in "${array_name[@]}"; do echo $element done
- **Concatenating Arrays:**
  - Combine two or more arrays.
    - combined_array=("${array1[@]}" "${array2[@]}")
- **Slicing Arrays:**

- Extract a portion of an array.
  - echo ${array_name[@]:0:2} (extracts the first two elements)

Sample Code:

```bash
#!/bin/bash

# Create an array
numbers=(1 2 3 4 5)

# Add an element to the end
numbers+=("6")

# Insert an element at index 2
numbers[2]="7"

# Remove the element at index 1
unset numbers[1]

# Iterate through the array
echo "Numbers:"
for number in "${numbers[@]}"; do
  echo $number
done

# Concatenate two arrays
colors=("red" "green")
other_colors=("blue" "yellow")
all_colors=("${colors[@]}" "${other_colors[@]}")
echo "All colors: ${all_colors[@]}"
```

This script demonstrates various array operations, including adding, removing, iterating, concatenating, and slicing elements. Arrays are a powerful feature in shell scripting that enables you to work with collections of data efficiently.

Chapter 8. Regular Expressions

Basic Regular Expressions
- **Definition:**
    - A sequence of characters that defines a search pattern.
    - Used to match and manipulate text based on specific patterns.
- **Basic Metacharacters:**
    - **. (dot):** Matches any single character (except newline).
    - ***** (asterisk): Matches zero or more occurrences of the preceding character.
    - **+ (plus):** Matches one or more occurrences of the preceding character.
    - **? (question mark):** Matches zero or one occurrence of the preceding character.[1]
    - **[] (character class):** Matches any single character within the brackets.
        - Example: [a-z] matches any lowercase letter.
    - **[^] (negated character class):** Matches any single character *not* within the brackets.
        - Example: [^0-9] matches any character that is not a digit.
    - **\:** Escapes special characters (e.g., \. matches a literal dot).
- **Anchors:**
    - **^:** Matches the beginning of a line.
    - **$:** Matches the end of a line.
- **Quantifiers:**
    - {m}: Matches exactly m occurrences.
    - {m,}: Matches m or more occurrences.
    - {m,n}: Matches between m and n occurrences.

Examples:
Find all lines containing the word "hello" using
grep "hello" file.txt

Find all lines that start with "http" using
grep "^http://" file.txt

Find all lines that end with ".txt" using
grep "\.txt$" file.txt

Find all lines containing a string of digits using
grep "[0-9][0-9][0-9]" file.txt

Advanced Regular Expressions

- **Grouping:**
  - (): Creates a group of characters.
    - (abc) matches the literal string "abc".
    - Groups can be used for backreferences (referencing previously matched groups).

- **Backreferences:**
  - \1, \2, \3, ...: Refer to the text matched by the corresponding group.
    - Example: \(\w+\) \1 matches two consecutive occurrences of the same word.

- **Alternation:**
  - |: Matches either the expression before or the expression after the pipe symbol.
    - Example: cat|dog matches either "cat" or "dog".

- **Lookaround Assertions:**
  - **Positive Lookahead:** (?=pattern): Asserts that the pattern must follow the current position, but does not consume any characters.
  - **Negative Lookahead:** (?!pattern): Asserts that the pattern must not follow the current position.
  - **Positive Lookbehind:** (?<=pattern): Asserts that the pattern must precede the current position.
  - **Negative Lookbehind:** (?<!pattern): Asserts that the pattern must not precede the current position.

- **Word Boundaries:**
  - **\b:** Matches the empty string at the beginning or end of a word.

Sample   Code:

```
# Find lines containing two consecutive occurrences of the same word
grep -E "\b(\w+)\b \1\b" file.txt

# Find lines containing either "cat" or "dog"
grep -E "cat|dog" file.txt

# Find lines that contain the word "hello" followed by the word "world"
grep -E "hello(?= world)" file.txt

# Find lines that do not end with ".txt"
grep -E ".*(?!\.txt)$" file.txt
```

regular expression features. Mastering these features allows you to create more complex and powerful patterns for text matching and manipulation.

Note: These examples use the -E option with grep to enable extended regular expressions. The specific syntax and features of regular expressions may vary slightly depending on the tool or programming language.

Using Regular Expressions with grep, sed, and awk

- **grep:**
  - **Basic Usage:** grep 'pattern' file
  - -E: Enables extended regular expression syntax.
  - -i: Ignore case.
  - -v: Invert the match (find lines that *do not* match the pattern).
- **sed:**
  - **Substitution:**
    - sed 's/pattern/replacement/g'
      - Replace all occurrences of pattern with replacement.
  - **Example:**
    - sed 's/\b[0-9]+\b/number/g' file.txt

- Replace all numbers with the word "number".

- **awk:**
  - **Pattern Matching:**
    - awk '/pattern/ { actions }'
      - Execute the specified actions only for lines that match the pattern.
  - **Field Extraction:**
    - Use regular expressions within field separators (e.g., -F '[,:]' to use comma or colon as field separators).

Sample Code:

```
# Find all lines containing the word "hello"
grep "hello" file.txt

# Find all lines that start with "http" (using extended regex)
grep -E "^http://" file.txt

# Replace all occurrences of "old_word" with "new_word" in a file
sed 's/old_word/new_word/g' file.txt

# Print only the lines that start with a vowel
awk '/^[aeiou]/ { print }' file.txt
```

This script demonstrates how to use regular expressions with grep, sed, and awk for various text processing tasks, such as searching, replacing, and filtering data. Mastering these tools allows you to efficiently manipulate text data based on complex patterns.

Chapter 9. Debugging and Troubleshooting

Debugging Techniques
- **echo Statements:**
  - ○ Insert echo statements within your script to print the values of variables, intermediate results, or messages to the console.
  - ○ This helps you track the execution flow and identify potential issues.

- **set -x:**
  - ○ Enables debugging mode.
  - ○ Displays each command before it is executed, along with its arguments.
  - ○ Useful for tracing the execution of your script step-by-step.

- **trap Command:**
  - ○ Allows you to execute commands before a signal is handled.
  - ○ Can be used to perform cleanup actions or display debugging information when the script receives signals (e.g., SIGINT for interrupting the script with Ctrl+C).

- **Using a Debugger (e.g., gdb):**
  - ○ For more advanced debugging, you can use a debugger like gdb (GNU Debugger).
  - ○ Requires compiling your script into an executable and then using gdb to step through the code line by line, inspect variables, and identify issues.

Sample Code:

```bash
#!/bin/bash

set -x # Enable debugging mode

# ... your script code here ...

# Example usage with trap
trap "echo 'Script interrupted by user.' && exit" SIGINT
```

This script demonstrates the use of set -x for enabling debugging mode and the trap command to handle the SIGINT signal (Ctrl+C). By using these techniques, you can effectively identify and fix errors in your shell scripts. **Note:** Remember to remove or comment out debugging statements and disable set -x before deploying your script to production.

Common Scripting Errors

- **Syntax Errors:**
  - Incorrect syntax (e.g., missing semicolons, mismatched parentheses, typos in commands).
  - Unmatched quotes.
  - Incorrect use of control flow structures (if-then-else, loops).
- **Logic Errors:**
  - Incorrect conditions in if-then-else statements.
  - Incorrect loop conditions.
  - Incorrect variable assignments.
  - Missing or incorrect calculations.
- **Permission Errors:**
  - Lack of permissions to read, write, or execute files or directories.
  - Attempting to modify files or directories without appropriate permissions.
- **Path Errors:**
  - Incorrect or missing paths to files or directories.
  - Using relative paths when absolute paths are required.
- **Variable Errors:**
  - Using undeclared variables.
  - Incorrectly referencing variables (e.g., missing $ before the variable name).
  - Variable scope issues (using local variables outside their scope).
- **Command Errors:**

- o Using incorrect command names or options.
- o Passing incorrect arguments to commands.
- **Debugging Tips:**
  - o Use echo statements to print the values of variables and intermediate results.
  - o Enable debugging mode with set -x.
  - o Check the script for syntax errors using a text editor or a linter.
  - o Carefully review the logic of your script.
  - o Test your script thoroughly with different input values.

Sample Code (Illustrating a Syntax Error):

```
if [ $a -gt b ]   # Missing dollar sign before 'b'
then
    echo "a is greater than b"
fi
```

This script contains a syntax error because the variable b is not properly referenced.

By understanding common scripting errors and using effective debugging techniques, you can write more robust and reliable shell scripts.

Troubleshooting Tips
- **Read Error Messages Carefully:**
  - o Pay close attention to error messages. They often provide valuable clues about the source of the problem.
  - o Look for specific error codes or messages that can help pinpoint the issue.
- **Check for Syntax Errors:**
  - o Use a text editor or a linter to check for syntax errors in your script.

- Look for missing semicolons, mismatched parentheses, incorrect quotes, and other syntax issues.

- **Debug with echo Statements:**
  - Insert echo statements throughout your script to print the values of variables, intermediate results, and messages to the console.
  - This helps you track the execution flow and identify where the problem might be occurring.

- **Use set -x:**
  - Enable debugging mode by running set -x before executing your script.
  - This displays each command before it is executed, along with its arguments, which can help you identify unexpected behavior.

- **Test in a Controlled Environment:**
  - Test your script in a controlled environment (e.g., a virtual machine or a sandbox) to minimize the impact of potential errors.

- **Break Down the Problem:**
  - If the problem is complex, try to break it down into smaller, more manageable parts.
  - Test each part individually to isolate the source of the issue.

- **Consult Documentation and Online Resources:**
  - Refer to the documentation for the shell you are using (e.g., Bash, Zsh).
  - Search for solutions online (e.g., Stack Overflow, Unix & Linux Forums).
  - Look for similar issues and their solutions.

- **Seek Help:**
  - If you are stuck, don't hesitate to ask for help from other experienced users or online communities.

Sample Code (Illustrating echo for debugging):

```bash
#!/bin/bash

# Calculate the sum of two numbers

read -p "Enter the first number: " num1
read -p "Enter the second number: " num2

echo "num1: $num1"
echo "num2: $num2"

sum=$((num1 + num2))

echo "The sum is: $sum"
```

This script includes echo statements to display the values of the input variables, which can be helpful for debugging if the calculation is not producing the expected result.

By following these troubleshooting tips, you can effectively identify and resolve issues in your shell scripts and improve your scripting skills.

www.ingramcontent.com/pod-product-compliance
Lightning Source LLC
LaVergne TN
LVHW051616050326
832903LV00033B/4528